# A LEAN AGAINST THE WHEEL

*Egon H.E. Lass*

FUTURECYCLE PRESS

*www.futurecycle.org*

Cover art, "Wrapped Figures," by Ronald Gardiner

Cover and interior book design by Diane Kistner

Book Antiqua text and Kolo LP titling

Library of Congress Control Number: 2015942350

Published by FutureCycle Press
Lexington, Kentucky, USA

ISBN 978-1-938853-78-4

*For Roni*

# Contents

1

Algae
Have taken over
The kelp forest.
Emperor fish

Are cruising around
Decaying fingers.
Before the body sank
A pair of eyes

Was cleanly picked away
By gulls,
But here the drowned
Pair,

Meaning
The body knew where to sink.

2

My youth
Is a German shepherd.
We sit quietly and listen
To the bickering walls.

I know the ghosts
Are flitting through them.
The dog disdains
All fiends

Smaller than the height
Of his acute ears;
He materializes
According to my needs.

I have forced him
To love me.

3

Those intertwining fingers
Above the armlets, wristlets,
Bands of solid gold,
Beneath those enigmatic eyes

Searching, asking, longing,
Opaquely subversive,
Those incomparably feminine hands,
Waking butterflies with one caress,

Where would they dare
To quest?
Would they not hazard
A tactful grab,

To raise (Mon Dieu!)
A flaccid member from the dead?

4

In the last shutdown,
When the post office was closed,
You had to mail yourself
By touch-screen.

Your destination was unclear
And there was a line
Impatiently accumulating behind you.
The scale rebelled,

Refusing to weigh
The amassed litter
Of your disorders.

Unless you lose them,
You will not be able to send yourself
Into the next possibility.

5

The heart of Socrates leapt
When he read in Anaxagoras
That mind arranges
And is responsible for everything.

The heart of Socrates fell
When there was no further explanation
And, on top of that,
The earth was flat.

Someone should have taken
Anaxagoras by the lapels
And told him to look up at the stars,
Or learn from Anaximander,

Who knew the earth to be round.
Urgently, we should also be told.

6

An agent is hiding
Behind the BMW.
He has been following me
For two weeks,

Talking into his right wrist.
My sister tomorrow
Was yesterday my wife;
Next week she has been,

I believe, an agent's lover
Who has just now and then
Will murder my doctor.

In full flight
I was not
Myself in any future.

# 7

That Hatti lay under his feet,
What of it?
And they wrote
That no miracle

Of equal worth
Had ever happened in Egypt,
As when Mat-Neferu-Re
Came with her army
To be the Pharaoh's wife.

But that no traveler
In the land of Syria,
Unto the river Euphrat,
Had fear in his heart,
That was the true miracle.

8

Poor stones,
Who are without experience,
Do not remember
The river's caress,

Are never ripe
Like pomegranates
Or figs;
Have no eyes to perceive

A flaming bush,
No tree
From which to drop
Into a field,

As I have dropped,
An apple, to the ground.

9

Beautiful Africa
Sits on a spoil heap.
"And maybe you, Amriki,
Maybe you marry me?"

She comes in the afternoon,
Nefertiti,
Waves away oceans
Or snow never seen,

The modern literate
Cities in the west,
No tears for extended family,

The enormous distance
That would never carry
Her cry for help.

10

You nod
A split second after
He or she nods.
You laugh

As if on cue,
Not of your own volition,
But because others
Have found amusing

What you did not understand,
Or missed,
Being located forever
At the other end of the room.

Although there is that other airhead
Who laughs at the same time you do.

11

When in your flesh-colored stilettos
With their blood-red soles
You stumbled at dusk
Onto the rotting boards

Of that pier,
And in a state
Of half insanity
I took you in my arms,

When your husband came
Lunging at me
And sailed off the edge
Into the polluted Atlantic waters,

Were we really acting
Like mature people, Cherie?

Summer, making
Not so upstanding
Sunrises
A few times in a row,

And fall, upset,
Flexing a bow
And shooting straight
Into summer's rectum.

The seasons feeling
Void
Except for an urge
At insurrection.

Nothing for harvest to do
But fling rotten tomatoes.

## 13

In my dream
Alexander at Issus
Actually caught the fleeing Darius,
Chopped off his right hand,

Had it cooked,
And ate it
In front of the Persian king,
Telling him

About the sumptuousness
Of human flesh.
All of the sources
Tell of no such thing,

And all of this
Is not necessarily true.

14

Vapor of gravity
Settling on window panes
At the very eastern edge
Of a latent sound wave.

The toe of a time-sock
Is pulled in
And out of itself,
To be folded up with a time-sock

From another universe.
The two are basically equal
Except for an occasional run
In the knitted plasma.

The universes
Are doing their laundry.

A room's atmosphere
Zigzags in whispers,
Pauses herringbone patois,
Saunters labyrinth argot.

A patriarch's whisper
Zigzags by tartan textile,
Pauses in argyle wheeze,
Saunters dogtooth patois.

A wish for the present paisley
Falls among polka dots,
Vanishes in pinstripe,

Unlike the Faire Isle moon
Where nothing falls
And no one stripes a pin.

16

It's not
As though you were
A marksman,
And she is wearing

Her superiority
Like an evening gown.
Her diamonds
Blink and strike

Dead center
Into your deficiencies.
Your bones disintegrate.

Nothing to do
But offer them to her
At discount.

17

I know a figurine
Of the goddess Tanit.
Three holes in her body,
Two of them plugged.

That is why
We must plug
The hands and feet
Of Jesus.

The power pouring
Out of those holes
Is too great.

The heat and the pain
Act upon you
Like a beam in the eye.

A hair on one head
Said to a hair on another head,
Look here,
You don't want to admit it

But there is under me
A tall and handsome fellow.
His armpit is honking
Seductive odor,

So formidable a weapon
That I am not at liberty
To tell you about it.

But look at you.
Soon you will depart
Because, frankly, your man is balding.

The trains are not going
To vanish therein,
And trying to stop them
Will be increasingly

Difficult.
Soon they will just
Keep running.
Chicago-Houston-LA.

And it will all
Fly out of your head,
The uncontrollable
Ticket-master

And your phantom love
Who jumped off the platform.

20

Truth,
Bereft and cast
Under a bridge,
Had been blinded

By a lie,
But charity found him
And took him home with her,
Enticing him

Into her bed.
The natural outcome
Was a multitude
Of sons and daughters.

Like healing ointment,
They have caused much pain.

The victim gunned down
In a poor suburb,
The judge is washing his hands.
We were all innocent,

But someone ratted
After the cock crowed.
There was no transport for the body,
So we stopped the Toyota

Of a guy from Cyrene
Under three crossed telephone poles
And held him with a Glock.

The alcoholic mom named Mary
Waited for three days,
But by then he was gone from the morgue.

Fie fie Madame,
Ready to savor with you
These infected escargots,
This rotted bar of salads

Like green frog cuisine,
The frog being
Of the enormous disposal kind,
In alleys where I have always

Been deemed worthy.
Assuredly,
My accommodating nature
Has no address

But would include occasionally
Dessert a-la-meth.

When happiness comes
You are careful.
You hide her
Behind the iceberg irises.

She is too exotic
A stranger,
Coming from nowhere
Like a crash victim.

Others may be jealous,
As though she were the mistress
That could not be controlled,

Coming and going unannounced,
Stolen and opened
Like someone else's birthday present.

24

There must have been
A northern version,
A lost account
Of how quasi-Centaurs

Battled quasi-Lapiths.
They left behind
A country of unripe fruit
And cold brooks

In which infants were held
Under water
To toughen them for future wars,

But causing only crises of identity,
Young men forever wondering
Whether they were human or fish.

Oxygen
Is a costly business,
Almost as expensive
As lust.

While we are getting
More and more entangled
With algae and fern,
Observe how life and death

Are maliciously grinning
From the face of the water.
There is a new tax
On breath and sight,

And someone is breaking your eardrums
Blowing retreat.

No way to play a war.
The heart of the king
Fell through his armor
When the white knight showed.

His queen, a fickle lady,
Was seduced.
She strode thoughtlessly
Into the battlefield,

Dispatched by a feisty pawn.
The rooks and bishops
Battled briefly
Among zigzagging knights.

Haughtily the king was no check
For a mate.

A shyting Bedouin
Is a bundle
Of half disrobed
And robins in a desert gully.

The only time
He looks more like his laundry
Than his sheep.
The horse and fruit flies

Half dead but not deterred.
The goats ate all the paper,
No sticks, no grass,
But stone.

Watch out
For snakes and spying walking sticks.

28

The eternally jealous Juno
Of son-in-law Hercules
Has become a modern shrew
In her popular

Reality show.
Feasting on his disasters
Supplied by accredited
Identity thieves,

She watches him burn
In self-inaugurated
Immolation,

Hoping by the Moirai
That he has covered her ass
With life insurance.

He was the classic type,
A one-eyed pirate
Missing half his teeth.
Before we drank our beakers

Comatose,
He offered me a slave,
A chocolate and honey
Woman from the south,

And I insanely,
In a moment of pure conscience,
Gave him my refusal,

As if the woman
Would be better off
In his bad company.

## 30

Leaving her servants behind
She wandered by the banks
Of mighty river Tigris
Where armies had battled.

From a buried warhorse
A swarm of hornets rose.
She slipped and fell
Into the waters,

Which took her out to sea,
And she washed up
On distant shores.

After long decay
Her spine became the deadly asp
That never stung Cleopatra.

It did not matter
That you ate among the villagers,
Picked fleas from your collar,
Shook in the same fevers,

Danced the stick dances
And parried jokes
In a common language.

They carried daggers
To their tribal councils
And plotted revenge.

Even in poverty
They remained warriors,
Preventing you forever
From understanding Africa.

It wasn't then
A colorless face,
Wasn't hollow-eyed
With uncared hair

Bleached, wasn't cracked
Lips
With sores and scabrous
Throat and hard,

Wasn't transparent
Skin with no bones
Sticking out
And no hanging breast,

Didn't look like
And was hunger.

To my surprise,
Charon knew nothing
About the shores.
All of them

Threw tentacles of life
Into the sea.
He could not take me
Where I wanted to go:

Into a peaceful existence.
The shores reeked
Of strife,
Threatening all who approached.

"Get off my boat!" he cried,
"You don't belong here!"

Having faced
The iron-tipped horns
Of fire-breathing bulls,
Ripped out the serpent's teeth

And used them for seeding a field,
Taken possession
Of a precious hoard
By outfoxing a dragon,

And before all this
Faced Scylla herself
In a North Atlantic hurricane,

What will you do
When a woman approaches you
And says, "My name is Medea."

From the Terranes
Across the Tethys Ocean
Going east
To Gondwanaland

Trees, brushes
Reeds, ferns
And none to devour them
Or each other,

Memory eastward
Wrapped in stone,
Nonchalant and nameless
For hundreds of millions of years,

At the very last moment
Named.

36

There is a slowness
In women of the sea,
A heaviness
To lodge a lean

Against the wheel.
There is a solidness
To words
From women of the sea,

Deep-hauled
From stolid combers
That manifest
From unseen swells beneath.

Possibly they have nymph
In their ancestry.

Abraham did not unfetter me
With mandatory esteem.
I sat with him
In his goat-hair tent,

Hagar behind the partition
Suckling Ishmael.
There was no narrative;
It was censored on high.

For a long time
We avoided the neon signs,
But a horizon approached
In which the goats ate credit cards.

He told me to leave
Because the ram refused to be victim.

After the crash,
Let my heart
Pump your blood.
I have left the shore

And sense the spring
In your breath
But cannot survive
Heartless.

Your raised wineglass
Is my bottle note
Carried by each wave.

Through a reversal of scope,
A mirror knows
My part in you.

All the red-chested warblers,
What is their confession?
Did they not as mortals,
And in frenzied hate,

Rip their own children apart,
Boil them in pots,
Roast them on spits,
And feed them to their husbands

As surely as Procne did
To avenge her sister?
And is not this beauteous
Bosom red

What remains
Of such ghastly feasts?

## 40

It would not do
To stand by the shore
Of Lake Kinneret,
To gather crowds

Upon that famous mountain.
In these particular days
Prophets depend on
Social media,

But as soon as Christ has posted
His world-saving message,
It is instantly obscured

By reams of toilet paper,
And by that
Which it usually wipes.

41

When Romans dismantled
The Western Wall of the Temple Mount,
You had ten- and fifteen-ton stones
Plummeting down forty meters

And smashing onto
The stone slab pavement below,
Smashing also into the sewers
Below the pavement;

Archaeologists attempting to investigate
These sewer tunnels,
Ripping their clothes
On sharp edges of collapsed stone,

Emerging from the underground
Buck naked.

# 42

When I rested my head
In her lap,
On the snowy sidewalk
By the train station,

She gave me to eat
Of her *terra rossa*
And promised to send
Not just ants,

But other creatures
To eat my body,
To clear my flesh
Of fiery bones.

She had about her
A democratic tenderness.

43

Swinging on a rope
Into a dark cavern,
South
Of the Temple Mount,

Which turned out to be
Cruciform,
And none had breathed the air
For two millennia.

The Nazarene who walked there,
Acclaimed by those
Who did not crucify him,

Could not apprehend
The cavern's shape
That would become his destiny.

## 44

He came last night
To my neighbor,
Who'd bombed himself
Sky-high.

His mangy cat
Took flight forthwith,
The ruddy dog
Jumped,

Stung by clairvoyance.
Ignoring syringes in filth,
The thief took
What was his.

I, sleepless,
Chewed over the neighbor's soul.

45

Ornamental flesh
Replete with absence,
Your second half
Burned into it,

Throw a lasso,
Catch yourself a chronicle,
Sieve it through water
And strain off

Singed laughter
But fill the maps with phantasies,
A world of cotton
For soft landing,

All the pointing fingers
Converged into one.

46

Impossible tomorrow,
Awake you come
In hibernation,

Yourself beyond,
Live to expect
No choice,

Yelling your nature,
Set and set
Abilities of all
The limit

Will not allow,
To go beyond
This DNA.
So courage.

47

Pumping steroids
Into his buttocks,
He becomes Hercules
And trounces the enemy.

Once there was a dog
Named Hercules.
He threw away his trifocals,

Growled like a bear,
And bit an octogenarian
In the ass.

His fur lies rotting
In a Second Avenue sewer;
His dentals chatter
And bite Greek ghosts.

48

As the wheel spins,
A *Glycymeris* shell
Is held against the side
To lay burnishing tracks
Down the vessel.

Like a voice recorder,
It has imprinted
The yelp of a crippled dog,
The din of children's voices
Onto the shining trail

And, very softly
In the background,
The plaint of the jar
Objecting to its creation.

## 49

Through breakers
In a schooner,
The enraged, white-bearded pilot
In his launch,

Screaming, "Starb'd!
Starb'd, you goddamned fools!"
The ship ripped around
On starboard tack,

And all her crew
Saved,
While the launch
Is tossed to the sky,

And of the pilot
Not a sign.

50

He used
Your long black hair
To weave the string.
Your body
Is a turquoise
Violin.

We all
Are woven strings,
And through the night
How gently
All the rushes
Sing.

You are the rushes,
I'm the bow.

51

The future remembered
Suddenly
That the past
Was unreliable,

The way it echoed
How time had passed.
The remembered future
Had shivered slightly

And warmed itself
In cascades
Of white-washed truth.
It breathed easier,

Because the danger
Was hiding in the present.

## 52

My father!
You,
On those distant Walda heights,
Where they blew you to shreds,

With enormous strides
In storm boots of death,
I come to lay
A twisted rag
At your feet,
My soul.

I already see you
Shrinking, thinking,
Who is this lunatic?
Is this my son?

53

See this here?
That's the end of the world.
I often dangle my feet
Off the ledge.

Down there, and to the left,
Appears to be hell.
I always thumb my nose
At the demons.

They can't quite make it
Up to the ledge,
But sometimes,
With long ropes,

I see people going down there,
For scientific purposes, they say.

Did relative things
Suddenly
Throw lightning
Into your eyes?

Did windows slam
And roof plaster fall
Onto the immaculate
Floors?

Were there
Strange knockings
On the front door
That made you look up in fright?

Did you, by any chance,
Think I was coming home?

If I were mother-
Of-pearl,
Swarthy divers
Would scoop me

From the forgotten reef
In a recollected ocean.
They would sell me
In scandalous marketplaces,

And my queen's servants
Would capture me
For a dirge.

Then I would shine
Upon her soft neck,
A chilly talisman.

The snake was disguised
As a king of carnivals.
Eve thought
It was going to give her

Enchanted worlds,
That the apple
Was magical.
She tasted it, thinking

That it would transport her
To a field of lucky stars
And dancing suns.

In this she deviated
From what God thought
Was going to happen.

When you think
About the innocent
Genius
Of Thomas Jefferson,

Possibly
There will be
A certain taste
Under the tongue.

The inescapability
Of history,
Your indulgence
Of the whole process,

And the taste of innocence
Changing under the tongue.

Punk Little
Red Riding Hood,
Wearing her
Crossfire and bone print

Off-shoulder mini dress
And lovelorn shlock
Skele-de-Hele flats,
Nonchalantly

Put her hands
Into her heartbreaker girl's
Biker hood pockets,

And totally
Freaked the wolf
With her dead dog skull pin.

A bullet smashes
Clean through its target
And careens uselessly
On.

A faucet is closed,
But the water
Keeps running for a while
Longer.

A flywheel is disengaged
But spins uselessly
Round and round.

A useful ignorance
Has ceased to be useful
But continues forever.

## 60

First I lay
Semiconscious
After the beating,
But then I began playing

With the other corpse
That you had left behind.
The blood
Was so thick.

I swished my fingers,
Leaving wide tracks
On the floor,
And bumped into the knife.

You had dropped it,
In your excitement, while beating me.

Like the smallest spark
Of a thousand bonfires
Is the snuffed eyelid
Of a sparrow.

Gentle animals,
Unschooled in complaint,
Die quietly like apples
During harvest time,

Hardly noticed
In the omnipotent space
Inhabited by death.

Within that space
The sound of whetting
Echoes up to the angels.

Long and short ago,
Those who yelled
String 'em up!
Became the beggars
For soup and mercy.

Long and short ago,
Within one breath,
The horse-drawn plow
Became a rocket
To the next celestial atom.

In waves and wars
Time blew away the clocks,
Awareness into void,
And Christmas into June.

In love forever and forever,
Marrying,
And doing the illogical,
Living together.

And she gets hooked
On too many lottery tickets,
And he goes bowling
Every night.

And she throws her dowry
At his head,
And he answers her
With his only treasure,

A china cabinet
Full of profanities.

64

Racing
Through the northern Sinai,
The endless waste of sand,
Broken by one Bedouin

Walking in the distance.
Making camp
In arbitrary space,
Somewhere

Between Arish and Qantarah,
We smelled a dark
Familiar smell

And in the morning
Saw the hands and feet
Protruding from the sand.

Mr. and Mrs.
At the church social
Told all the ears
Along the limestone wall

Their concept of authenticity;
Dressed it up
Chapter and verse,
Proving the truth of the truth.

Meanwhile the universe,
Sedate in its billions of years,
Did a double take,

Changed direction in midcourse,
And accommodated itself
To the newly stated reality.

66

The right eye
Sending e-mails
To the left.
It was lost in a war

And is now amber.
All inbox messages
About the two feet,
One deployed to an IED,

Address unknown,
Still flying
Between a thumb and a paper bag
Under transparent skin.

That branch of evolution
Was lost in the encrypted jungle.

67

When the mountains
Turn red,
When the owl
Goes hunting,

The blue shirt
Once again
Endures the daily spillage
And drool.

The black pants
Are stained
In a bathroom.

At bedtime
Both of them vomit
Their occupant.

## 68

Many days
I waited for your message,
And when it came
My breath was restored.

Then I began reading
And thought
That someone had handed me
A snakeskin,

A surface
Ground bare of color.
The next time you see me,

I shall be a husk
Extravagantly offering you
My emptiness.

## 69

Who made this word
Anyway?
The constituents
Are too unimportant.

What can you do
With a p or an s?
I'm the fourth one
In this row,

And there is indeed
A sense intuition
Of meaning.

Don't breathe or move.
Who knows what will happen
If we cross over.

70

Impossible to read
You.
The hair-you
Has never seen

Its labyrinthine equal.
The mouth-you
A separate organism
Projecting desire.

The ear-delicate
You. What trails
Have the melodies left?

The comedy-you,
The tragedy-you,
Singly, but too much at once.

Come to the corner café.
I shall be wearing
My skin
Of glorious victorious defeat,

My banana-peel
Shirt and trousers,
Under my hat
Languishing

All the betrayed
Betrayers harmonizing
With the melancholic
Angel of Death.

Whatever you do,
Don't come with the usual answers.

## About FutureCycle Press

FutureCycle Press is dedicated to publishing lasting English-language poetry books, chapbooks, and anthologies in both print-on-demand and ebook formats. Founded in 2007 by long-time independent editor/publishers and partners Diane Kistner and Robert S. King, the press incorporated as a non-profit in 2012. A number of our editors are distinguished poets and writers in their own right, and we have been actively involved in the small press movement going back to the early seventies.

The FutureCycle Poetry Book Prize and honorarium is awarded annually for the best full-length volume of poetry we publish in a calendar year. Introduced in 2013, our Good Works projects are anthologies devoted to issues of universal significance, with all proceeds donated to a related worthy cause. Our Selected Poems series highlights contemporary poets with a substantial body of work to their credit; with this series we strive to resurrect work that has had limited distribution and is now out of print.

We are dedicated to giving all of the authors we publish the care their work deserves, making our catalog of titles the most diverse and distinguished it can be, and paying forward any earnings to fund more great books.

We've learned a few things about independent publishing over the years. We've also evolved a unique, resilient publishing model that allows us to focus mainly on vetting and preserving for posterity the most books of exceptional quality without becoming overwhelmed with bookkeeping and mailing, fundraising activities, or taxing editorial and production "bubbles." To find out more about what we are doing, come see us at www.futurecycle.org.

## The FutureCycle Poetry Book Prize

All full-length volumes of poetry we publish in a given calendar year are considered for the annual FutureCycle Poetry Book Prize. This allows us to consider each submission on its own merits, outside of the context of a contest. Too, the judges see the finished book, which will have benefitted from the beautiful book design and strong editorial gloss we are famous for.

The book ranked the best in judging is announced as the prize-winner in the subsequent year. There is no fixed monetary award; instead, the winning poet receives an honorarium of 20% of the total net royalties from all poetry books and chapbooks the press sold online in the year the winning book was published. The winner is also accorded the honor of being on the panel of judges for the next year's competition; all judges receive copies of all contending books to keep for their personal library.

www.ingramcontent.com/pod-product-compliance
Lightning Source LLC
Chambersburg PA
CBHW070009100426
42741CB00012B/3173